150 HAPPY FACTS

by The Happy Broadcast

Mauro Gatti · Keith Bonnici

Andrews McMeel
PUBLISHING®

150 Happy Facts copyright © 2023 by The Happy Broadcast.
All rights reserved. Printed in China. No part of this book may be used
or reproduced in any manner whatsoever without written permission
except in the case of reprints in the context of reviews.

Andrews McMeel Publishing
a division of Andrews McMeel Universal
1130 Walnut Street, Kansas City, Missouri 64106

www.andrewsmcmeel.com

23 24 25 26 27 TEN 10 9 8 7 6 5 4 3 2 1

ISBN: 978-1-5248-7577-0

Library of Congress Control Number: 2022940056

Made by:
1010 Printing International, Ltd.
Address and place of production:
1010 Avenue, Xia Nan Industrial District,
Yuan Zhou Town, Bo Luo County
Guangdong Province, China 516123
1st printing – 9/12/22

Editor: Erinn Pascal
Designer: Tiffany Meairs
Production Editor: Brianna Westervelt
Production Manager: Tamara Haus

ATTENTION: SCHOOLS AND BUSINESSES
Andrews McMeel books are available at quantity discounts with bulk
purchase for educational, business, or sales promotional use. For information,
please e-mail the Andrews McMeel Publishing Special Sales Department:
sales@amuniversal.com.

Hi There =)

Let me tell you a little story about The Happy Broadcast.

www.TheHappyBroadcast.com

The year was 2018. If you landed on Earth from a different planet and read or watched the news, you would have thought that the world was a terrible place.

The news was so focused on the negative things happening, that it was easy to miss all the many positive things going on.

That is when artist and creator Mauro Gatti decided to use his talents to try to spread positivity.

Mauro began to draw the good news and share it on social media. He drew about animals being saved from extinction, illustrated news about new technology helping the environment, highlighted news about people taking action to plant entire forests, and many more real world news events that showed positive actions being taken to improve our world.

Before long a movement was born. Millions of people began to follow, share, and comment on the many wonderful things that Mauro was bringing to light with his drawings.

A few years later, Mauro met Keith Bonnici, a fan who was fascinated by the way that Mauro was able to build such a vibrant community around positivity.

Mauro and Keith quickly became friends and began to talk about how positivity can be so powerful in helping improve someone's happiness. After some time, the two joined together and went on a mission to try to improve the mental health of as many people as they could by promoting positivity.

In early 2021, the two decided that reading positive news alone was not enough and that more could be done.

That is when they began to work on a mental health and wellness project called WHOLE. A short while later they launched the WHOLE mobile app, a place where people can maintain a positive outlook and participate in a number of science-backed activities that can help boost their mental health and happiness. WHOLE is great for people of all ages and helps you keep a positive outlook. Give it a try… it's free!

www.GetWHOLE.co/download

Today, both The Happy Broadcast and WHOLE are places that people spend time engaging with positivity while working together to improve their own mental health, which collectively can help impact the world and the many wonderful creatures in it.

150 Happy Facts is part of our journey to promote positivity and improve mental health. We hope you enjoy some of the many positive things happening in our world through the drawings of Mauro Gatti.

1. There are already 10 countries whose electricity comes from 97% to 100% renewable energy sources.

Costs for renewable energy continue to decline each year as technologies continue to develop and become more efficient. Albania, Bhutan, Democratic Republic of the Congo, Costa Rica, Ethiopia, Iceland, Namibia, Nepal, Norway, and Paraguay are countries whose electric power generation comes from 97 to 100% renewable energy sources.

Countries are using a variety of renewable energy sources. Scotland, for example, is very heavy on wind and has managed to get to 90% renewables. Kenya gets 44% of its power from geothermal, whereas in Albania most of the power comes from hydroelectric, which is relatively cheap, reliable, and can be generated any time of day in any season.

Moving toward 100% renewable energy sources will become easier over time, as wind, solar, and other renewables become more efficient and battery storage technologies become capable of storing larger quantities of energy for use when needed.

2. One school in Maryland is sending kids to meditation, not detention!

In a move that changes the way children are disciplined in schools, Robert W. Coleman Elementary School in Baltimore, Maryland, has established its "Mindful Moment" program, which sends children to a mindful moment room when they misbehave. Children sent to the mindful moment room are then given the opportunity to stretch and practice yoga and meditation, with the aim of encouraging them to wind down and relax in the face of stressful situations.

The program was created through the school's partnership with a nonprofit organization called "The Holistic Life Foundation." The room includes a staff member who helps the children work through the issue that has caused them to misbehave. The success of the program is evident, and school principal Carlillian Thompson says that he now rarely has to speak to students over disciplinary issues!

Environment

3. New carbon capture facility in Scotland will remove one million tons of CO2 from the air each year.

In a breakthrough moment for carbon capture technologies, a new facility set to open in Scotland will remove up to one million tons of carbon from the air each year. That is the equivalent carbon that would be absorbed by 40 million trees! The facility will be the largest in the world, and all the absorbed carbon will be deposited in storage sites under the sea.

The new facility joins a host of other carbon capture technology innovations aimed at meeting the requirement of reducing the amount of CO2 in the atmosphere to reverse the adverse effects of climate change. As the Union of Concerned Scientists (UCS) points out on its website, "to reach net-zero emissions, we need to do more than just reduce our emissions: we need to actively remove carbon dioxide from the atmosphere or offset its effects."

4. A new study shows that if you want to live longer, you should be around a green space!

Researchers have found that green spaces are correlated with improve-ments in mental health, immune function, and metabolism. Green surroundings help us reduce stress and connect with others, according to the study, and they offer a haven from traffic noise, better air quality, cooler temps, and a place for people to be physically active. Half of the world's population lives in urban environments, so making sure that those people have exposure to more green spaces may produce positive benefits for public health.

5. Did you know? Blueberries are packed with vitamins to help reduce anxiety.

When we're anxious and stressed, our bodies crave vitamin C. Small but mighty, blueberries are bursting with antioxidants and vitamin C, which have been shown to provide anxiety relief. Blueberries can help regulate and prevent spikes in cortisol levels by repairing and protecting cells damaged by the stress hormone. This helps to calm nervous disorders such as anxiety.

Blueberries also combat stress by boosting serotonin levels (serotonin can be called "the happy hormone") and regulating our brain function, which helps counteract depression and anxiety.

6. Nepal is on track to become the world's first country to double its wild tiger population since 2010.

Nepal is one of 13 countries that pledged to double the number of tigers in the wild as part of an initiative known as TX2. To date, Nepal is on track to double its wild tiger population from a 2010 statistic.

How did they do this? A tough anti-poaching approach and close engagement with communities living near tiger habitats is the key driver behind Nepal's accomplishment of this important goal. As an added benefit, the measures taken by Nepal in connection with TX2 have also had a positive effect in boosting the populations of other species, including rhinos and elephants.

7. There's a new tool to help those who have suffered from heart attacks—drones!

In 2021, a 71-year-old Swedish man had a heart attack while shoveling snow. He is alive due to the quick action of a drone!

Shortly after his heart attack, a nearby doctor programmed a drone to fly in a defibrillator, which saved his life. Typically, someone having a heart attack needs help within 10 minutes to survive, and in this case, Everdrone's Emergency Medical Aerial Delivery (EMADE) service allowed emergency dispatchers to send a drone carrying the device to the doctor's location.

It took three minutes to deliver the defibrillator to the man's home and a nearby doctor on the way to his job used the device on the patient after providing CPR. Currently, the EMADE service can reach 200,000 Swedish residents and the company said it plans to expand to more locations in Europe this year.

8. What's the secret to a better yoga session? Cats! Purr-fect!

MarySoul Yoga is a yoga studio in Milan, Italy, that organizes cat yoga classes. Eleanora Coco, the owner of the studio, noticed how much her students loved having her cat, Musa, around during yoga sessions, which caused her to experiment and offer lessons with four-legged friends in her studio.

The studio owner believes that cats absorb negative energy and release positive energy. Many students of her yoga classes have said that doing cat yoga has helped them forget about their stress.

The yoga sessions with cats also have a separate noble purpose: adoption! Many of the "yoga cats" are looking for a family, and one of the main goals of the project is to show how great the cats are to try to find them a home.

9. Humpback whales made a comeback in 2021!

The humpback whale, a species that was listed as endangered just 25 years ago, is making a comeback. Recently, as many as 500 humpback whales—and a record 21 whale calves—were documented in the Salish Sea, according to the Pacific Whale Watch Association (PWWA).

Twenty-one new calves represent the highest annual number so far in the region and is nearly twice as many as were reported in 2020, which only documented 11. Researchers believe there are more than 21,000 humpbacks now in the eastern North Pacific and as many as 85,000 worldwide. The 21,000 in the North Pacific is up from about 1,600 when whale hunting was banned in 1966. Humpback whales are now of little concern in terms of being endangered!

10. Martin Luther King Jr., who was the youngest person to receive a Nobel Peace Prize, donated all the prize money to organizations that aided progress of the Civil Rights Movement.

The Rev. Dr. Martin Luther King Jr. was one of the most visible and influential figures in the Civil Rights Movement. But did you know that, at age 35, Dr. King donated his Nobel Peace Prize money to charity?

The incredible activist, leader, and changemaker received a Nobel Peace Prize for his commitment to civil rights, nonviolence, and helping the US government move toward making discrimination unlawful. His prize included a check for $54,123, which he didn't keep but instead donated to various organizations that were working to create progress through the Civil Rights Movement. Thanks, Dr. King!

11. Scientists have created an enzyme that breaks down plastics speedily.

Plastic pollution is one of the biggest environmental problems on our planet. Thankfully, a team of engineers and scientists at the University of Texas have created an enzyme that can break down plastics easily. Typically, plastic waste takes centuries to degrade. With this new intel, the same plastics might break down in a matter of days—or hours!

Of course, matter is never created nor destroyed, so the project was able to break plastics down and then put them back together. This suggests that the enzyme has the potential to dramatically aid the process of *recycling* so that major industries will be able to reduce their environmental impact by recovering and reusing plastics at the molecular level. Talk about good news!

12. The government of Wales will gift each household a plant!

Evidence has long shown that trees have positive environmental and social effects. Some benefits include helping to reduce carbon emissions, but evidence also shows that being around trees helps people reduce stress and lower blood pressure.

Because of this, the government of Wales announced a program: each household in their jurisdiction gets a free tree to plant! Residents have a choice of native species to plant in their gardens, or, if they do not have a green thumb of their own, to have a tree added to the woodlands on their behalf.

In total, about 1.3 million trees were made available by the Welsh government over the course of 12 months starting in March 2022.

13. Icelanders celebrate Christmas by reading!

Iceland is a nation of book lovers! A study from 2019 showed that the average Icelander reads 2.3 books per month. This trend likely traces back to the tradition called *Jolabokaflod* (translated in English as "the Christmas book flood"), which started during World War II when paper was one of the few things not rationed due to the war.

During Jolabokaflod, Icelanders give books as gifts. Today, people all over the world are now encouraged to celebrate Jolabokaflod by gifting books on Christmas Eve and setting aside Christmas to drink hot cocoa and read.

14. Doctors in Japan are now prescribing "forest bathing," or spending time in nature!

When humans spend time in nature, there are many positive mental and physical benefits, like reduction of anxiety and depression. That is why in the early 1980s, a public health program called *shinrin-yoku*, or forest bathing, was started. It combats growing mental health issues among the Japanese population.

Forest bathing involves a person going into nature and being present with all five senses. The use and presence of technology is discouraged (i.e., patients must turn off their phones), and patients often bathe with bare feet for a full grounding effect.

Since the launch of shinrin-yoku, it has become a part of the Japanese healthcare system. Forest bathing has been shown to lower patients' heart rate and blood pressure, improve mood, and decrease fatigue, anxiety, and confusion. Increased forest coverage has even been suggested to lower overall mortality rates!

15. No lonely funerals! In the Netherlands, if you die without any family to attend your funeral, an organization will send a poet to read a custom poem at your service.

Frank Starik, a Dutch artist and poet, created The Lonely Funeral Project, an organization whose goal is to make funerals a little less lonely. The poet does research about the deceased and creates a poem memorializing their life. This is done when the person who died has little or no family and helps make sure they aren't forgotten.

Starik's poems are read at the funeral, typically held with a group of pallbearers, a designated civil servant, and the poet. Lonely Funerals bring comfort to the living in the idea that there is always someone looking out for us.

16. Conservationists in South Africa sent 30 white rhinos to Rwanda to ensure the survival of the species.

Thirty white rhinos have been sent to and settled in a national park in Rwanda. Weighing up to two tons, the majestic animals were transported as part of a program to replenish the species' population. In what Africa Parks called "the largest single rhino translocation ever undertaken," the 30 rare white rhinos include 19 females, 11 males, and a mix of adults and adolescents.

According to the national park regional manager, this provides an opportunity for a safe rhino environment in Rwanda.

17. A blood test using RNA markers is offering new hope to people with depression.

Researchers from Indiana University performed a study that showed it's possible to create a blood test for depression and bipolar disorder that can match people to the right medications. How does the test work? When stressed or depressed, certain hormones and other trackers are released and affect a person's blood and immune system. Researchers studied the biological basis of mood disorders and succeeded in developing a tool that can help in distinguishing them from these hormones and trackers in the blood.

The ability to detect these psychological ailments with a blood test can help doctors prescribe the most appropriate medications and reduce the time it takes to diagnose potentially serious mental health issues. That's reason to celebrate!

18. The Great Barrier Reef is bursting with new life as millions of "coral babies" are born.

The Great Barrier Reef was left damaged in 2016, 2017, and 2020 due to heatwaves. However, some good news—billions of coral babies have been born on the Great Barrier Reef off the coast of Cairns, Australia, since then. Coral spawning happens once a year, so a good coral baby season is something to celebrate.

19. Landmark HIV vaccine passes phase 1 human trial and proves successful in 97% of the participants.

HIV affects more than 37 million people worldwide. It's one of the most difficult viruses to target with a vaccine, mainly because of an unusually fast mutation rate that allows it to constantly grow and avoid the human immune system.

However, there's a breakthrough new vaccine approach for the prevention of HIV and it's shown significant promise in phase 1 trials. The vaccine is able to target the desired immune cells and could become the first stage of a multistep vaccine strategy to fight HIV and other diseases. The targeted response of the trial vaccine was detected in 97% of participants who received the vaccine, which is a great sign toward eventual success of the product. The study sets the stage for additional clinical trials that will seek to refine and extend the approach, with the long-term goal of creating a safe and effective HIV vaccine.

20. In a first for the world, a Swedish food brand opened a grocery store where products are priced based on their climate impact.

In terms of climate impact, food production is responsible for about a quarter of the world's greenhouse gas emissions.

Despite consumers wanting to make better choices about the food they eat and its effect on the environment, it can be difficult to know which foods are best for the environment. Swedish brand Felix is providing clearer guidance with its new The Climate Store, a food store where customers pay for products that are priced based on their climate impact. The company states that to cut our climate impact in half, every customer must stick to a weekly budget of 41.7 lbs (or 18.9 kilograms) of carbon dioxide equivalents. This is a great example of a company taking climate change seriously and helping to empower people to make better choices for the environment.

21. Scotland's First Minister reassured children that Santa would not face COVID-19 restrictions on Christmas Eve because "he's an essential worker."

In 2020–2021, a lot of the world was shut down with tight travel restrictions because of the COVID-19 pandemic. As Christmas drew closer, kids were worried about whether Santa would be unable to travel too. But the Scotland government reassured everyone that Santa would not face any restrictions when he delivered presents on Christmas Eve.

  In a time when the world was so isolated because of a serious virus, it was nice to see a government doing something to reassure kids and help reduce the impact of COVID-19 on their mental health and happiness.

22. Great news! Giraffe populations have rebounded by 20% since 2015.

Research shows that the giraffe population has increased across Africa. Reports estimate that the world's giraffe population is currently around 117,000, a 20% increase since 2015.

Did you know? Giraffes were once considered to all be part of a single species, but recent genetic testing shows that there are likely four species of giraffe. Three of these species have increased considerably in population, while the fourth, Southern giraffes, have plateaued.

The survey of giraffe populations was collected across 21 countries, by governments, researchers, nonprofits, and scientists.

23. Virtual reality can help with therapy!

While therapy is a long-trusted method that has helped countless people improve their mental health, many have resisted therapy as they are scared to discuss their feelings with a doctor. For those who find opening up to a therapist too daunting, you are not alone. As an alternative to in-person therapy sessions, a recent study found 30% of people prefer to talk about negative experiences with a virtual reality avatar, rather than a person.

This means that therapy might soon be opened up to new people who don't feel comfortable with traditional face-to-face interactions.

24. The last Saturday of every month, Rwandans get together to volunteer for community improvement projects.

Umuganda is a national holiday in Rwanda. Each month, it takes place on the last Saturday. On Umuganda, Rwandan citizens do nationwide community service work for four hours, such as build schools and hospitals or help rehabilitate wildlife. The entire country shuts down to take part in the government-mandated community service day.

An estimated 80% of Rwandans take part in this monthly community workday. From 2007 to 2019, Umuganda's contribution to Rwanda's development has been estimated at more than $60 million USD. Way to go, Rwanda!

25. Doctors in Canada can now prescribe time in nature, such as a trip to a national park, to help with people's mental health as part of their new mental health plan.

Similar to the Japanese practice of forest bathing, doctors in Canada are now able to prescribe time in nature as part of a patient's mental health plan. The BC Parks Foundation has partnered with Parks Canada and created the prescribe nature initiative (PaRx).

National park passes are made available for health-care providers to "prescribe" nature to patients dealing with both physical and mental health challenges. Prescriptions range from time outside in local parks to year-long Parks Canada Discovery Passes, which cover admission to more than 80 parks across the country.

26. Romania wants climate change education in schools to enable students to learn more about the challenges the world faces from climate change.

The president of Romania launched a 141-page proposal to include climate change education in regular school curricula. The proposal aims to increase the amount of climate change and environmental education that students receive, creating a national network of 10,000 environmental "mini inspectors," supporting nature-based activities, and creating digital learning materials on climate change.

Beyond the early education component of the plan, longer-term goals include improving the sustainability of school infrastructure and cutting schools' carbon footprints in half by 2030. Plus, kids feel a deeper responsibility for the environment. Win-win!

27. All non-eco-friendly car ads in France will soon show warning labels. The message will include environmental warnings and promote green alternatives.

Car advertisements in France must soon provide information to people about eco-friendly transport options. The new law seeks to clamp down on the country's air pollution by educating people about the many alternative options whenever a car company advertises.

The law requires car companies to pick one of three slogans to include in all TV, radio, print, and online advertisements including, "on a daily basis, take public transport," "consider carpooling," or "for short journeys, walking or bicycling is preferable." Car companies must also use the hashtag #SeDéplacerMoinsPolluer, which means "move and pollute less." Companies who fail to include the environmental warning will face fines of up to $60,000 USD per advertisement.

28. Scientists in Singapore have produced a new kind of cooking oil from microalgae that can serve as a healthier and greener replacement to palm oil.

One of the most widely consumed vegetable oils is palm oil. However, some studies have linked palm oil to environmental and physical health concerns.

A new algae oil innovation presents a possibly healthier alternative to palm oil that is also better for the environment. What's more, microalgae oil can lower an individual's risk of heart disease and creates a smaller carbon footprint than palm. Say it with us: yay for algae!

29. To combat the environmental impact of electronics manufacturing, Austria now offers a $250 stipend for those who repair old electronics instead of buying new ones.

The environmental impact of most consumer electronics is highest when they are manufactured, so anything that can reduce the need to create new electronics would dramatically reduce the impact of technology on the environment. Austria is trying to reduce the need for new electronics manufacturing by encouraging people to repair old devices instead of replacing them.

The Austrian government is offering a "repair bonus" of up to $250 USD for people who hold on to their old devices and repair them. This covers large household appliances like fridges, washing machines, dryers, and coffee machines, but also items like computers, mobile phones, electronic toys, and power tools.

Each time we extend a gadget's lifetime, we space out and slow the environmental impact of manufacturing, which helps the environment. The fewer new items we buy, the more we limit greenhouse gas emissions, save water, and avoid using minerals that are hard to mine and harder to recycle.

30. Judge Ketanji Brown Jackson became the first Black woman member of the United States Supreme Court.

Congratulations to Ketanji Brown Jackson for being confirmed by Congress to a seat on the US Supreme Court!

Justice Jackson was nominated by President Joe Biden and is the 116th justice in US history. She received bipartisan backing, with a final vote of 53 to 47 in the Senate, and is the first Black woman to sit on the highest court in the United States.

What a powerful moment in the history of the United States and a reminder that change can come!

31. An Airbus A380, one of the largest passenger planes in existence, successfully completed a flight powered by sustainable fuel derived mostly from cooking oil.

Flying in the future might be possible using cooking oil for fuel! In 2022, a test flight in Toulouse, France, confirmed this data.

An Airbus A380 performed the first-ever flight powered completely by Sustainable Aviation Fuel (SAF). The fuel was derived mainly from cooking oil and other waste fats. SAF is a fuel that has the potential to reduce lifecycle emissions by up to 80%, compared to conventional aviation fuel.

Currently, all Airbus aircraft are certified to use up to 50% SAF mixed with kerosene, but experts hope to achieve 100% SAF flight certification before 2030.

32. France has banned the long-time practice by fashion brands of burning their unsold stock, leading to labels donating them or discounting them instead.

High-end fashion brands have long kept their products at a premium price through a practice that involved them burning unsold items. However, a groundbreaking new law in France makes destroying unsold goods a criminal offense that could result in financial penalties or prison time. This new law will require luxury companies to manage their inventory. It also encourages companies to make donations or recycle goods.

33. A blind inventor developed a "Smart Cane" that uses Google Maps and ultrasonic sensors to identify surroundings.

An estimated 250 million people are visually impaired, according to the World Health Organization. Now, thanks to the genius work of a blind inventor named Kursat Ceylan, people who lack sight can more easily navigate the world with the use of his invention, the Smart Cane.

The Smart Cane, also called the WeWalk cane, uses ultrasonic sensors to warn its user of nearby objects and obstacles by vibrations in the cane's handle. Not only can the cane be paired with a smartphone's Bluetooth system for easy control but it also works with voice assistant and Google Maps software. What an amazing use of technology!

34. Lebanon green-lit the world's first hospital to serve its patients 100% vegan food to aid in their recovery.

A hospital in Lebanon has identified that a plant-based diet is a natural step in the recovery of its patients. It has become the first hospital in the world to serve vegan-only meals.

Around the world, other hospitals are also starting to do similar things. For example, San Francisco, California, is moving toward a reduction of animal products in public hospitals. While the Lebanon hospital is the only hospital that has completely stopped offering animal products, other hospitals are moving toward more plant-forward models. Pass the lentils, please!

35. Sea otters hold hands with their loved ones while taking a nap so they do not drift apart as they sleep.

Want some *otterly* adorable news? A published article explores the reasons why sea otters are often seen holding hands while they sleep. You see, sea otters sleep on their backs while floating in the water, usually somewhere near the shoreline where the water is calmer. However, the constant current of the body of water can still result in them moving. So, to avoid drifting apart and potentially losing one another while sleeping, the animals hold hands. What a cute and practical way to keep your family together!

36. Kopenhagen Fur, the world's largest fur auction house, will close as demand for animal pelts drop, marking the beginning of the end for the global fur trade.

Kopenhagen Fur, the world's largest fur auction house, plans to shut down by 2023, starting what could be the end of the global fur trade.

Kopenhagen Fur has long acted as a broker for furs produced in Denmark and around the world. The disappearance of this fur broker is likely to reduce the demand for fur products in countries all over the world.

37. Cities and communities around the world are starting a dog DNA database to analyze pups' poop and track owners who don't clean up after their pets!

Some cities around the world are tracking down dog owners who don't pick up their pet's poop using pet DNA tracing. That's right, samples from poop left on sidewalks is being traced to find the owners who left it there, which can then lead to fines for the pet owner. How is the program being implemented? Some buildings are requiring pet owners who live there to swab their pet's cheek to create a database of the pet. Then, any time pet waste is seen on the premises, it is tested and traced back to the owner, who is then fined. While it is currently a small-scale operation being adopted by some buildings, the opportunity for it to grow is large. Clean sidewalks mean happy residents, so clean up after your pet!

38. Goodbye, gas. Norway's electric cars sell better than those powered by fossil fuels.

Norway is trying to become the first nation to end the sale of fossil fuel–powered cars. To reach that goal, Norway has exempted electric vehicles from taxes.

In addition to the reduction in taxes on electric cars, Norway has no sales tax, low tolls, no road tax, and free public parking for the vehicles, with charging points located throughout the country. In 2021, almost 65% of new cars sold were electric.

39. The first "retirement home" in Europe for elephants from zoos or circuses opened in France.

In 2021, a 52-year-old Asian elephant named Gandhi, originally from Thailand, moved to a new sanctuary called Elephant Haven. Elephant Haven is located in Bussière-Galant, France; it is a sanctuary for retired zoo and circus elephants.

The sanctuary was created in response to France's ban on using wild animals in circuses. The founders of the sanctuary want to create homes for more elephants and help them live the rest of their lives in peace.

40. A Canadian company aims to plant one billion trees using drones that shoot seeds into the ground.

To combat climate change, the Canadian company Flash Forest has an unusual solution: it will use drones to plant one billion trees!

The drones shoot tree seeds into the ground. Then, Flash Forest combines technology, software, and science to improve traditional tree-planting and quickly help global reforestation efforts. They intend to plant eight different species to make sure they create a healthy ecosystem.

The company's drones can plant trees ten times faster than humans can. This is helpful especially in areas that are hard to get to by other means of transportation, and more cost-effective, too.

41. In Switzerland, it is illegal to own just one guinea pig; they must be raised with companions so they do not get lonely.

While we have all heard about laws that fight against animal cruelty, have you ever heard of one that fights against animal loneliness? In Switzerland, it is illegal to own just one guinea pig, citing research that says the animals travel in herds and can get lonely when left without a companion. Two is better than one!

42. A nature fund in Australia purchased the last available commercial fishing license and retired it, creating a net-free haven for marine wildlife.

The World Wide Fund (WWF) for Nature in Australia purchased and retired the last commercial fishing license in the region, which creates a 63,000-mile (100,000-square-kilometer) refuge where marine life can be free from commercial fishing nets. Dolphins, turtles, and all sorts of other sea creatures can now swim freely in the area without the risk of getting caught in a commercial fishing net. This represents an innovative way for a conservationist organization to achieve their goal while operating within the existing legal framework, which can often be much faster than trying to change the laws altogether. Kudos to you, WWF!

43. In the wake of high gas prices, more eco-friendly transportation options are seeing a sales boom.

The COVID-19 pandemic and higher gas prices have both contributed to the boom in sales of electric bikes. The pandemic caused people to invest more in outdoor sports equipment, and now higher gas prices are helping boost e-bike sales as people switch to a more affordable form of electric transportation. The cost of owning a car is estimated to be around $10,000 a year and, while an e-bike isn't a cheap purchase, the long-term cost of ownership is dramatically lower due to lower maintenance and fuel costs. Plus, they sure are fun!

44. Solar power keeps on growing! There are now enough solar panels installed in the world to power all of Europe.

The world has reached a major milestone in solar as there are now enough solar panels installed to generate one terawatt of electricity from the sun. That represents enough wattage to power all of Europe. The European Union currently generates around 4% of its electricity needs from solar power, but estimates predict that solar power will account for roughly 20% of the European energy mix by 2040. Other countries are contributing to the solar revolution as well, with China, Europe, and the US together accounting for more than half of installed solar capacity globally. Record growth was seen in 2021 for home installations of rooftop solar panels and all trends are pointing in the right direction.

45. A new law in Panama grants nature the "right to exist and regenerate," meaning the government now has to respect the country's ecosystem in all future projects.

In 2022, Panama recognized the legal rights of nature. The law creates rights extended to nature, including the "right to exist, persist, and regenerate its life cycles," the "right to conserve its biodiversity," and the "right to be restored after being affected directly or indirectly by any human activity."

With this law, Panama joins a number of other countries in creating laws that give nature legal rights similar to those held by humans, corporations, and governments.

46. Kids can make a difference! Inspired by their students, two teachers launched a positivity hotline that offers pep talks provided by children.

The free hotline is called Peptoc and was receiving up to 700 callers per hour within two days of launching. It is a project from students at West Side Elementary in California and was put together by teachers who say they were inspired by the positive attitudes of their students. Despite the hardships of the COVID-19 pandemic and recent wildfires in the region, the students still approached their day with such positivity, which the teachers say impacted those around them. The idea is that getting a dose of positivity from these Peptoc conversations would help improve the moods of callers.

"The children's creativity and resourcefulness is something that we need to emulate, because that level of joy and love and imagination is what's going to save us in the end," the teacher said.

The hope is that the Peptoc pre-recorded messages will give callers a positive break from whatever hardship they are going through. Peptoc's number is 707-998-8410 (a US number).

47. TreeCard is the world's first debit card that plants trees, as a percentage of its profits are reinvested in reforestation projects around the world.

Many adults love their credit card rewards. The usual rewards are cash back on purchases or airline miles that can be used to buy airplane tickets, but a new debit card in the US allows users to donate money to environmental causes simply by using the card to pay for things. The debit card allows users to make contactless or mobile payments and cash withdrawals from banks and ATMs, and does not have a fee. Here's how it works: Each time it is used, the card company makes some money from fees the store accepting the card has to pay, and a portion of these fees (80%) are then transferred to be used to plant trees via a partnership the card company formed with Ecosia. The card is called TreeCard, which is fitting since using it allows you to plant trees!

As an added environmental bonus, the TreeCard itself is unique because it is made from sustainably sourced cherry wood—a single tree can create 300,000 cards. Using wood to create the card means that they do not have to use plastic, which takes a very long time to decompose. Win-win!

48. Baby alert! North Atlantic right whales, a critically endangered species, had a big baby boom recently.

North Atlantic right whales gave birth in greater numbers than usual this year. Three years ago, scientists were worried when the species produced no known offspring. This year, they saw the biggest boom since 2015! A total of 17 newborn calves were spotted by survey teams between Florida and North Carolina.

49. Some courtrooms across the US are employing trained dogs to take the stand alongside child abuse victims and comfort them as they testify about their experiences.

Child abuse is a very sad and scary thing, and victims are often scared if they have to testify about their experiences in a courtroom. To help reduce the stress of testifying in court, a growing number of courts in the US are allowing specially trained dogs to sit with the child while they are in court as a witness, which helps to calm them and make the process a bit easier. These children are brave heroes for helping to take bad people off the streets, and the pet companion helps make the experience of testifying in court a little less stressful.

Supporters say the dogs have made a huge difference in helping victims and witnesses open up on the stand, as they make them feel calmer while they tell the story of what happened. The use of these courtroom dogs is growing: As of 2022, at least a third of active courthouse facility dogs have assisted in the courtroom.

50. Friends make our life better (and longer)! A new study reveals that female giraffes live longer when surrounded by female friends that help with raising children and reduce harassment from males.

We all suspect that friends help make our lives happier, but new research on giraffes actually shows evidence of that.

Giraffes in the wild can have a pretty hard life, as they are crowded by humans and often threatened by poachers. A recent study showed that female giraffes who had friends around them can live longer and be happier. The study examined female giraffes in Tanzania and noted that they live longer if they spend time with large groups of other females. These "friends" are actually more important to their survival than even food availability, the presence of humans, and other factors. Why? Well, the study suggests that female giraffes are able to share information about the best food sources and work together in caring for their babies. They can also provide comfort when harassed by male giraffes.

51. The Japanese government has appointed a "Minister of Loneliness" to combat mental health issues.

Mental health and happiness issues have always been a concern, even before the COVID-19 pandemic hit. However, the pandemic made it worse as job losses, social distancing, and other factors created a more isolated society. Having a normal social life stopped by a pandemic is not an easy thing to deal with, and it created a lot of feelings of hopelessness in those trying times.

The Japanese government appointed an actual government position dedicated to helping with this loneliness crisis. Immediately upon being appointed to the role, a Japanese minister announced plans for an emergency national assembly to discuss the problem and share thoughts about how best to fix it. While sadness is always something that will be around, the fact that governments are focusing on trying to limit it is a positive sign that should be celebrated. Good work, Japan!

52. Plogging is a fitness trend that originated in Sweden and means to pick up litter while jogging. It not only takes care of the environment but it keeps the "ploggers" healthy, too.

A new fitness trend that tackles two worthy causes is getting some publicity. Plogging, which is the term used to describe the practice of picking up trash while you exercise, suggests that while people go for a walk/jog/run, they collect garbage along the way. This is a great way to get people to exercise more (which is good for their health) while also using that exercise time to do something good for the environment (picking up trash).

Another benefit of plogging, it doesn't cost much at all! The only equipment you need are some workout clothes and something to put the trash in as you pick it up along the way.

In terms of the exercise benefits, plogging is better than just walking or running since it incorporates squats into your workout as you bend down to pick up the trash you see. If you are looking for a new way to stay in shape and help the environment, try plogging!

53. All aboard! In an effort to cut back on carbon emissions, France voted to ban short domestic flights in favor of train travel if the trip can be taken in 2.5 hours or less.

In France, a trip from Paris to Lyon, for example, would take only two hours on a fast train, and therefore will not be offered via air travel in the future.

Those who support the flight ban say that traveling by train can often be cheaper and faster when factoring in the time it takes to get to the airport and move through security. Not to mention there is a significant reduction in carbon emissions on trains compared to planes!

54. The first human-composting funeral home in the US offers an environmentally friendly procedure that turns bodies into healthy soil.

Death is a sad thing that many of us do not like to think about, but a funeral home in the US is giving people a way to contribute to the environment in a positive manner even after they pass on. Traditional cremations and burials cause environmental damage because of the space and materials they use. Recompose, a company in Seattle, has opened the first human-composting funeral home where human remains are turned into soil that can be used to help generate new forest growth for the environment.

The company "uses the process of 'natural organic reduction' to gently convert human remains into soil," which is then turned into a productive fertilizer. Family members can then choose to keep the soil or donate it to a conservationist organization focused on restoring forests. The forest restoration project families can choose to donate to welcomes family members to visit and see the real impact their loved one has made, which can be a peaceful thing to do as a way to remember their lost loved one.

55. A Brazilian parachutist has dropped 100 million seeds from 27 species of native trees while parachuting over a remote and deforested area in the Amazon.

A Brazilian skydiver has performed one of the most important jumps of his life! Over the Amazon Rainforest, he carried more than 100 million seeds from 27 species of native trees while jumping over a remote deforested area in the heart of the Amazon. The seeds were sprayed out while he was parachuting down, in an effort to revive the heavily deforested area.

   The parachutist was diving at a rate of over 180 miles per hour and released the seeds at the exact height and location needed to maximize the impact. The seeds used for this feat have a germination rate of over 95%, so in a few years we should see amazing growth from the effort. What a thrilling contribution to the environment!

56. In 2022, Spain became the first western country to offer "menstrual leave" for employees.

The Spanish government is working to acknowledge menstrual pain as a legitimate medical issue. Under the proposed plan, employees who suffer from severe period pain can take up to three days off per month as a result. Studies estimate that, worldwide, over 60% of people with a uterus suffer from severe period pain, and the plan is intended to benefit those suffering from particularly painful periods. The leave policy is a formal acknowledgment of something that has long been ignored and hopefully sets a trend for other countries to follow.

57. An album of songs from rarely heard endangered birds has hit the top of the music charts in Australia, pushing out albums from Mariah Carey and Michael Bublé.

Songs of Disappearance is an album filled with the sounds of cockatoos, bowerbirds, seabirds, and night parrots, and it debuted in Australia in early December 2020, rising to the top of the charts.

The album is different from other holiday music albums because it only includes the sounds of recorded bird songs and calls. The album is said to include sounds made by 53 of Australia's rarest birds, many of which are almost extinct.

The album is not only something cool to listen to but it is meant to remind us all of the wonderful things that could be lost if we do not take care of our wildlife and environment. As an added benefit, all profits from the album's sales are being donated to Birdlife Australia to help support their work of conserving the natural environment and numerous species of birds.

58. New Zealand launched an initiative to encourage recycling. Anyone who does a great job recycling gets to show off a gold star on their recycling bin.

Even adults like getting gold stars! So, the recycling council of Christchurch, New Zealand, launched an initiative to encourage households to do a better job at recycling.

Households that put the right items in the right bin get a gold star for their recycling bin, which the neighbors can see. It has become a way to publicly recognize those doing a good job, which pressures others to step up their game. Those households who do not do a good job of recycling get a warning letter before their bin is then taken away. The result of this new program has been great! Recycling rates have improved and now over 80% of contents in bins are able to be processed and recycled. Rewards can go a long way to motivate people to put in the extra work! Great idea, New Zealand!

59. Great news! Giant pandas are no longer an endangered species. Thanks to conservation efforts, their numbers are finally rebounding after years of decline.

Until recently, giant pandas were endangered and on a path toward extinction. That is no longer the case as a movement to push reproduction efforts in zoos as well as reforestation and conservation campaigns has helped. In fact, so much progress has been made that the panda's status has been upgraded from endangered to vulnerable. They are not out of the woods yet, but the momentum is much more positive after people came together to care for the species.

While the numbers of pandas in the wild are still small, in China they have increased from 1,114 in the 1980s to 1,864 in a recent survey. Other than pandas in the wild, protected panda habitats have doubled in size, protecting 66.8% of giant pandas. After decades of work, it is clear that the survival of pandas will depend on further efforts by humans as we work to battle the impact of climate change and deforestation of their natural habitat.

60. Big news for the big cats! In a major move, South Africa will finally ban the breeding of lions in captivity for trophy hunting or for tourists to pet.

Hunting lions is a practice that has been common in South Africa for a long time, and the industry also included breeding lions for hunting purposes. Fortunately, this practice will end as South Africa has decided to ban its captive lion industry. The cruel practice of raising lions to then be hunted for their fur and bones, or as a means of providing a sport to tourists, has been the target of conservationist groups for years, and it looks like the battle has finally been won!

Respect for the lives of animals is the mark of an evolved society, and as humanity evolves, we are seeing more and more rules put in place that protect animal life. Progress is hard and often slow but should be celebrated regardless.

61. Scotland makes history as the first country in the world to provide free menstruation hygiene products!

Scotland has passed a bill that makes menstruation hygiene products, such as tampons and pads, free to all who need them.

The law, first passed in November 2020, requires local authorities to make these products generally available to women and all people with uteruses without charge. Schools and colleges must make sure they are available to students, and designated public places must also offer them for free. Access to basic hygienic products is a positive thing for governments to focus on, and Scotland is the first country in the world to provide them for free.

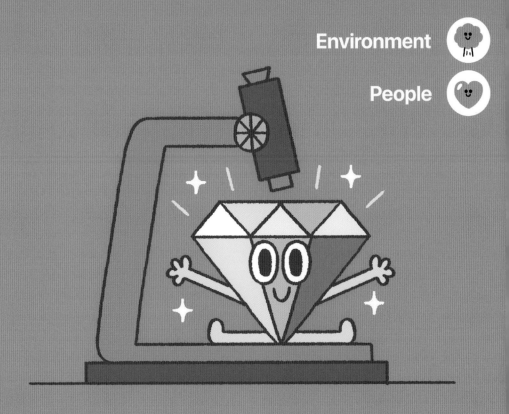

62. The diamond industry is now focusing on more sustainable, lab-grown gems.

In recent years, manmade diamonds have become a growing alternative to natural diamonds. Pandora, the largest jewelry maker in the world, has announced that it will no longer use mined diamonds in their jewelry. Pandora also announced that the company's diamonds will be grown using 60% renewable energy, with the goal to be 100% within a year. The company is also committed to using more recycled silver and gold.

Corporate responsibility at its finest!

63. Amsterdam metro stations ban advertisements encouraging fossil fuels.

People passing through Amsterdam's busy metro system will no longer see ads for gas-powered cars and cheap flights, as these environmentally damaging products will no longer be allowed to display advertising there.

This particular ban will impact the many large-screen TV ads that play to an estimated four million passengers that use the metro each week, and the hope is that the initiative is one of many that neighboring cities and countries will adopt and build upon. Responsible advertising can help shape consumer behavior and improve our overall approach to how we care for the environment.

64. Wildlife success story! Californian porpoises have more than tripled their population.

Laws make a difference in helping to promote policies that can save the environment. In this case, a law banning a certain use of fishing nets has led to a revitalization of a dolphin population that was once in danger.

In the past, fishermen used low-cost nets that sit like fences on the floor of the ocean. These nets were highly effective at catching fish as the mesh snags the fish by their gills. While helpful to provide fish for food supply, these nets also catch a lot of other species by mistake. One of these is the harbor porpoise, which have seen a dramatic increase in their population since the ban went into effect. Harbor porpoise populations have grown by over 8,000 in number around the world. A great win for our sea life, so the next time you see the amazing sight of dolphins jumping out of the water on our coastlines you will know why.

65. Oil company Shell will cut its CO2 emissions nearly in half by 2030.

A Dutch judge has ruled that Shell Oil, one of the companies that some say is most responsible for the world's carbon emissions, must cut CO2 emissions by 45% and meet Paris climate goals.

   The court ruled that Shell must factor in all the cars, trucks, and planes that burn its fuels when it slashes its carbon emissions. The court also held that the oil industry confused the public about the science of climate change and lobbied lawmakers to loosen climate laws.

66. Great news for our beloved bees! The European Court of Justice has rejected an attempt by a chemical giant to overturn a ban on bee-killing pesticides.

No bee-killing chemicals here! Chemicals that interfere with the homing systems of bees who pollinate crops will remain banned in Europe. Harm to the homing system made it impossible for the bees to find their way back to the hive, causing the bees to die. But no more!

In 2021, the court upheld the ruling and rejected the manufacturer's final attempt to overturn the ban, which was put in place for the protection of the environment and human health, said Greenpeace.

Hooray for bees!

67. Glasgow, Scotland, tackles climate change with trees!

Good news! A new forest will be planted in and around the city of Glasgow and will include 18 million trees. The forest will be named the Clyde Climate Forest and will have 10 trees per resident. It is part of the city's commitment to raise the area that is covered by trees from 17% to 20%.

The team behind the project aims to plant trees on former coal-mining sites, land that is vacant and in poor condition, urban streets, and rural areas that were once filled with tree cover but have been de-wooded over time.

68. A new study found that 120 minutes in nature a week is all that it takes to increase self-esteem, reduce anxiety, and improve mood.

Nature is good for you! A recent study conducted at the University of Exeter noted that, out of 20,000 people, those who spend two hours a week in green spaces are more likely to report good health and well-being. The study saw this positive health data reported across the board, regardless of occupation, ethnicity, economic status, and other characteristics of the participants.

Research is proving that nature is good for your health, which will hopefully lead to new health initiatives aimed at bringing nature into people's everyday lives.

69. A new California law requires grocery stores and other food suppliers to donate all edible food waste.

Finally, a common-sense approach to food supply management! A new California law enacted in 2022 requires supermarkets and grocery stores to donate all edible food they would otherwise have wasted. This is not only a good thing for the planet as it makes more use of resources instead of wastes them, but it is also good news for people who are suffering from food shortages. In terms of the planet, less food waste means less garbage. For the homeless and others suffering from food shortages, not throwing away this food can hopefully increase food availability to them.

70. Sweden created an agency to combat fake news and the widespread problem of online misinformation.

The news that people consume plays a large role in shaping their way of thinking. That is why the existence of inaccurate, or "fake," news is a global problem as it can lead to misinformation skewing people's beliefs in a harmful way. In response to this problem, the government in Stockholm, Sweden, created the Swedish Psychological Defense Agency to help fight the spread of fake news. Fake news can "create anxiety, heighten hatred and doubt, and make society more vulnerable," says the agency.

People who repeat misinformation online are often unaware that the information is inaccurate. That is why it is important for all of us to be critical of sources and do our own research before sharing news we see with others. Sweden is not the only country trying to tackle this problem, as several European countries have changed or added to their fake news strategies.

71. Berlin Metro is offering metro tickets with hemp oil for stressed commuters. These daily tickets have a "calming effect" when eaten.

Edible bus tickets that help reduce stress? That is what Berlin's public transport company (BVG) is saying. Hemp oil is believed to have characteristics that can help relax the body and reduce anxiety. That is why BVG began offering public transport tickets with hemp oil added to them, which it says will have a "calming effect" if eaten. The tickets cost around $10 USD and are made from edible paper and are sprinkled with "no more than three drops" of hemp oil.

BVG says the oil is obtained from the seed of the cannabis plant, which, unlike the flowers of the plant, does not contain any intoxicating substances. The company says that the oil on the tickets is "completely harmless to health" and "completely legal."

Taking public transportation can often be a very stressful thing and this is an interesting way to try to reduce that travel anxiety.

72. In Spain, a law now recognizes pets as legal family members and a pet's welfare and feelings will be considered in divorce cases.

Divorce is a difficult thing for everyone involved, even pets! Spain has now started to consider a pet's welfare when couples get divorced. This is a shift in the law and strengthens the case for separating couples to get shared custody of their pets. Spain is not alone, as France and Portugal also require judges to consider pets in such situations. Pets are seen by those countries as sentient beings, not objects, which makes it easier to consider their wellbeing when resolving disputes as to ongoing care following a couple's separation.

   In the past, disputes over who got a pet in the divorce/separation was based on who "owned" the pet, but now a judge has to determine where the animal will have better wellbeing. A person who can show that they have the ability to best support the pet has a better chance of getting custody. Also, if there are children involved in the divorce, custody is likely to go with wherever the kids go, as there is a special bond between children and family pets. In a difficult time like divorce, it's nice to know that a pet's happiness is also being considered.

73. A United States nonprofit is training barbers to be mental health advocates and support their clients' wellbeing.

Mental health issues are a rampant problem in society that all too often go untreated. That is why a new idea by a nonprofit to train barbers to be mental health companions has the potential to have such a positive impact. Most men get a haircut four to six times per year. They spend 20 minutes or so in a chair while their barber cuts their hair. That time can be used to help engage customers about their mental health, which can help to destigmatize the topic and even potentially help provide some emotional support.

"America's First Mental Health Barbershop Movement" is a nonprofit organization that uses barbers across the country to connect with men and raise awareness about mental health. Through a 12-month teaching program, barbers are trained on techniques like active listening, understanding emotions, and how to use positive language to support positive mental health.

The Black community is largely impacted by the mental health crisis, and the founder of the nonprofit chose barbershops as a place to start because they are one of the few places in the Black community where everyone from all socioeconomic backgrounds can be found and a place where conversation is often already a big part of the experience. A great idea for a great cause.

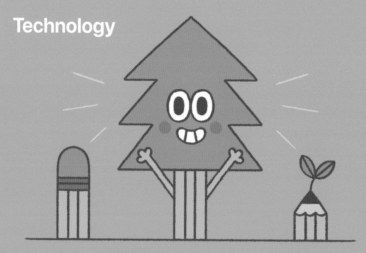

74. A Danish company lets you grow trees or plants from pencils. Their biodegradable pencils, which contain seeds, can be planted once you are done using them!

Did you know that we use 14 billion pencils each year at a cost of 82,000 trees that are cut down to make them? A Danish startup has come up with a new idea to help replace the trees we use in making our pencils. The idea: growing trees from pencils. That's right, a company called "Sprout World" has created the world's only plantable pencils. The pencils are made from wood and use lead made from 100% natural and non-toxic graphite. Not only are they environmentally friendly in how they are made, but also in how they are disposed of, as hidden at the end of the pencil is a plant-based capsule filled with seeds. Once you are done using the pencil, you can plant it into one of many seed options like tomatoes, flowers, or even a Christmas tree!

In just seven years the company has sold more than 30 million pencils to buyers all over the world. Great work!

75. Singapore is the first country to give the go-ahead to meat created without killing any animals, after approving the sale of lab-grown chicken nuggets.

The world's meat industry has historically been one of the largest polluters, not to mention the negative animal rights consequences that many people feel the industry represents. In recent years, however, there has been a revolution of plant-based meat alternatives, and now lab-grown chicken nuggets have been approved for sale in Singapore. The meat is produced without the slaughter of an animal as it is grown in a lab from cultured cells using a proprietary process created by a company called Eat Just. The development has been hailed as a landmark moment across the meat industry. Wahoo!

The product passed a safety review by the Singapore Food Agency and the approval shows glimpses of a future where meat is produced without the killing of livestock. The cells for the product are grown with plant-based ingredients and adds to Eat Just's offerings, which also has a vegan egg product that is sold in thousands of stores worldwide.

76. A New Zealand couple gifted land worth millions to the nation for "the benefit and enjoyment of all New Zealanders."

A New Zealand couple has gifted over 2,000 acres of land by the edge of a beautiful lake to the government for the benefit of its citizens. The couple turned down numerous offers from land developers that would have netted them millions of dollars, and instead gifted the land to the Queen Elizabeth II National Trust for "the benefit and enjoyment of all New Zealanders."

The couple's family has owned and worked on the land for 100 years and wanted to see it protected and loved for another century, rather than having it developed into condos or homes.

77. Istanbul, Turkey, there are vending machines that dispense food and water for stray dogs and cats when you recycle a plastic bottle. Everyone's a winner!

Curfews and lockdowns imposed in Turkey during the COVID-19 pandemic made it more difficult for stray animals to find food. To combat this, Turkey implemented "mamamatiks" (the Turkish word for vending machines) for animals. The machines meet the nutritional needs of stray animals, and people can recycle plastic, glass, or metal in exchange for credits which can then be used to dispense food and water for stray animals from the machine.

78. José Alberto Gutiérrez, a garbage man from Colombia, has been collecting books that were thrown away for 20 years. Now he has opened a free community library filled with 25,000+ books!

In Colombia, local children often stopped going to school and started working early because they couldn't afford books. José Alberto Gutiérrez, a garbage man who lives in Bogotá, began collecting books that were thrown away over 20 years ago, and today, the entire ground floor of his house is filled with more than 25,000 books. He has turned this collection into a community library called *La Fuerza de las Palabras* (Spanish for "The Strength of Words") and it has become an important place for kids in his community.

There is also a plan to add a new building location for the library in the future. Truly a way of turning another person's trash into treasure!

79. A startup is using artificial intelligence in supermarkets to dynamically change prices, reducing food waste by 40%!

Food waste is a real issue, and in the United States up to 40% of food ends up in landfills.

A startup called Wasteless thinks new technology called "machine learning" can play a role in helping to solve this issue. The company has developed a system for automatically reducing the price of food items as they spend more time on store shelves and get closer to going bad. The closer a food item gets to its "best before" date, the cheaper its price will be. The technology tracks dates of food item expirations and adjusts the price tags accordingly.

A store that ran a test with Wasteless technology reported nearly 30% less overall waste. The company believes it will do even better than that over time.

80. Fifty-four of the world's leading cities are on track to cut their greenhouse gas emissions.

Climate change is a well-known issue, but there is some good news as a new report shows that 54 of the world's leading cities, including Mexico City, Milan, and Paris, are now on track to help keep global temperature increases below target. The report goes on to say that these efforts by cities will prevent at least four trillion pounds of greenhouse gas emissions being released into the atmosphere over the next 10 years, which is equal to five times the annual emissions of the entire United Kingdom.

Activities helping to reduce the rate of climate change include mass tree-planting, new public transport networks, and other innovations that are being made to help achieve the goals set by the Paris Climate Accords.

The work to reduce the impact of climate change continues as almost 400 cities have committed to reaching net-zero emissions by the year 2050.

81. The European Parliament voted in favor of phasing out caged animal farming in response to a petition signed by 1.4 million EU citizens.

The European Union has just passed an initiative that aims to phase out the practice of caged farming over time. Over 1.4 million EU citizens signed a petition to ban the practice and parliament voted by an overwhelming majority to agree.

Hopefully this leads to more sustainable and humane animal farming practices.

82. New Zealand asked people around the world to share a regret or upset from 2020 online, and then welcome the new year with a "seed of hope" by donating a tree to build a new forest.

The year 2020 was a very difficult one for many people, with the COVID-19 pandemic causing most events to be canceled. Weddings, sporting events, concerts, and more were all practically nonexistent as most countries had strict lockdown and social distancing measures in place to protect populations from the spread of the coronavirus.

The country of New Zealand tried to turn lemons into lemonade, however, and asked people from around the globe to share their misfortunes from 2020 online. For every disappointment shared, others are invited to put a positive spin on by donating a tree for what is called the "Forest of Hope." This new forest of native trees would represent hope and regrowth for the new year ahead.

Turning misfortune into hope for a cleaner future sounds like a great plan!

83. There is a GPS tracker to keep the world's only known white giraffe safe.

The only known white giraffe in the world has been given a GPS tracking device to help protect it from poachers. The device allows rangers to track the rare giraffe's movements. The giraffe is white because of a rare genetic condition called leucism, and it is the only giraffe in the world with the condition. Good news—it will now be safe!

84. In one week, hundreds of people in Indonesia helped clear 110 tons of plastic off local beaches.

In Indonesia in January 2021, hundreds of people continued cleanup efforts at a beach on the island of Bali, after tons of waste washed up on the beach from celebrations that took place on New Year's Eve.

Thirty tons of plastic was cleared from the beach by New Year's Day, and by January 3, over 80 tons had been cleared from three beaches. The country had 600 local employees come in to help and at the end of the project over 110 tons of plastic was removed, which is equivalent to the weight of over 50 cars!

Trash on our beaches often finds its way into the ocean and causes harm to fish, turtles, and other sea life. By picking it all up before it made its way into the water, these people have saved the environment from loads of harm. A nice reminder of how important it is for us not to litter!

Environment

 People

85. The Mental Health Foundation in London has launched an initiative that will provide people experiencing poor mental health access to wetlands as a form of therapy. Nature as prescription!

A recent project showed that people with anxiety or depression improved their mental health by spending time in the wetlands. A new program in the UK offers six-week courses on the wetlands and includes activities like birdwatching, nature walks, and habitat protection work, designed to help expose people to the beauty and relaxing characteristics of the wetlands.

The next time you are feeling sad or stressed, try taking a trip to a nearby ocean or lake—it can help!

86. Germany and France are set to become the world's first countries to protect male chicks in the egg industry.

In the chicken industry, male chicks are often seen as worthless since they do not produce eggs and their meat is often not desired by those who eat chicken. In a ban enacted in 2021, Germany and France will no longer allow the mass slaughter of male chicks and will require animal farmers to use technology to manage their animals.

Technology can determine the sex of a chick while it is still inside the egg, allowing farmers to prevent male chicks from hatching in the first place. Additionally, to make sure that the unborn chick does not feel pain, farmers will be required to identify the gender early in the incubation process before it can sense pain.

This is a small step in the evolution of humanity to be more humane in how we manage nature and our food supply.

87. To defeat a rat infestation, the Tree House Humane Society shelter in Chicago has released 1,000 feral cats.

Rather than using poison or traps to try to solve a rat problem, the city of Chicago has decided to let nature help. Through a program called Cats at Work, an animal shelter is releasing cats onto city streets to help stave off the rodent problem. Cats are a natural predator to rodents, so the hope is that they can help reduce the rodent population in a natural way.

The cats that are being released are ones that "would not thrive in a shelter or home environment" and so, rather than having them locked up for a long period in an animal control center, they are being returned to the streets and helping solve a city problem.

While the cats will sometimes kill rats, that is not the goal; rather, the very fact that the cats exist is meant to scare off rats so that they are not a noticeable nuisance.

88. According to research, when you are kind to someone else, your brain releases feel-good chemicals that give you a feeling of happiness.

Giving is often even better for your happiness than receiving.

It may sound strange since when we think of acts of kindness, we usually think about how they benefit the recipient, but studies have shown that the giver of the act of kindness often receives as great a benefit. Random acts of kindness have been shown to release dopamine, a chemical in the brain that can give us a feeling of happiness. Research goes on to show that not only does helping immediately improve our brain chemistry, but it also has long-term impacts as the act of continued volunteerism is shown to impact people's life span.

Why? In short, the act of giving kindness lowers stress levels, which can reduce the risk of all sorts of health problems like high blood pressure and heart problems.

No matter how you choose to help, giving back is a win-win.

89. Germany hopes to grow its bee population with more than 100 wildflower meadows.

Bees are one of the most important creatures in the world. Their activities in pollinating plants are essential to the survival of many plant species. That said, bee populations have declined dramatically in recent years, posing a threat to their existence.

In Germany, hope is growing for wild bees and insects thanks to wildflower meadows that are being planted to reverse declines in insect populations.

More than 100 flowers and wild grasses have been planted throughout Germany's largest cities over the last three years, a good start to reverse the trend of declining bee populations. Germany has set aside $2 million to seed and nurture more than 50 wild gardens over the next five years. The city of Munich has also joined the process and established about 30 meadows. There are similar efforts in many other cities across Germany.

There is still plenty of work to be done to save the bees, but this is just one of many examples of things being done to help!

90. The last female Swinhoe's turtle (the most endangered turtle in the world) died in 2019, leaving the last male without a mate. However, researchers found another female in 2021, renewing hope for avoiding extinction!

Swinhoe's turtles are giant softshell turtles and were once thought to be certain to go extinct when the last female of the species died in 2019. The species was pushed to the brink of extinction, largely by hunters who used the turtles' meat and eggs. In a bit of good news, however, researchers have discovered another female turtle, meaning that there is still a chance to save the species.

Here's hoping this newly discovered female can bring new young turtles from the species to life!

91. A record number of people signed up to take part in the "Veganuary" challenge to eat a plant-based and climate friendly diet in January.

In 2021, an estimated 500,000 people signed up to the January vegan challenge, which is the highest number since the Veganuary challenge launched in 2014. Veganuary is a nonprofit dedicated to motivating people to try a vegan diet for the month of January, which they hope can lead to people discovering that veganism is something that they can do all the time.

Adopting a plant-based diet is one of the best things that people can do to reduce their environmental impact, as the process of producing meat is one of the largest producers of greenhouse gases.

A recent report suggests that pledging to Veganuary has resulted in saving 6.2 million liters of water and 3.4 million animal lives. Little changes by many people can make a big difference to the wellbeing of our animals and environment.

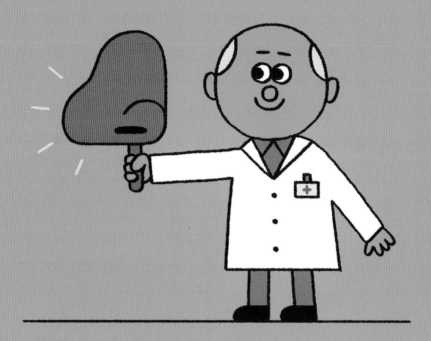

92. Researchers have developed a portable AI-based device called "E-Nose," which may one day be able to diagnose Parkinson's disease by smelling a patient's skin.

Parkinson's disease is an ailment that can lead to loss of muscle control among other symptoms. There is no cure for Parkinson's disease at this time, but early medical intervention can help make some of the symptoms more manageable and prolong the life of those who suffer with it. That is why getting an early diagnosis is important, but historically it has been hard to discover Parkinson's until the disease has progressed.

Some recent good news is that researchers have developed a portable "e-nose" that they hope could someday diagnose the disease by smelling a patient's skin. The device works by detecting an odor that has been found in people with Parkinson's. Apparently, Parkinson's patients have a higher-than-normal amount of sebum (an oily substance produced by our glands) and so being able to detect these higher levels could signal that a patient has the disease. In early tests, the e-nose was found to be 70.8% accurate in correctly identifying who had the disease.

While finding a cure is the ultimate goal, early detection can help patients, so the invention of the e-nose is a positive step forward.

93. Scotland's forests are the largest they have been in over 900 years, with an area that went from 6% of land coverage to 18%.

According to data from researchers at Our World in Data, Scotland's forests have recovered to the point where they are as large as they have been in almost 1,000 years. That's right, a place where forests are actually thriving and not shrinking! In the past, about half of Scotland's forests were lost due to deforestation, but renewed efforts by the government to curb climate change led to a reversal of that trend. And the best news is that the country is not done yet, as the government has a target of 21% forest coverage (meaning 21% of the country's land would be covered in forest) by the year 2032.

94. During the early days of the Russian invasion of Ukraine, a German pianist traveled to the border to play his piano for refugees as they entered Poland to escape the war.

In times of struggle, it is often the little things that humanity does that make all the difference. As millions of refugees were fleeing the Russian invasion of Ukraine in March 2022, a musician used his talents to try to improve the situation of others. He traveled to the border of Ukraine and Poland (over 5,000 miles away from his home) and began to play his piano for refugees as they crossed the Polish border.

Among the pain and suffering of war, there are occasional heartwarming stories that give us hope for humanity. The musician said of his playing, "They leave the bombs behind and they go to the music."

95. After 60 years of conservation efforts, the humpback whale is no longer a threatened species!

A triumphant win after 60 years of effort, the beautiful sea creatures are no longer on the "threatened" list. At the lowest point, there were thought to be as few as 1,500 humpback whales left in Australian waters, but after huge conservation efforts that population is now thought to be over 40,000 in the area. And the number is growing!

Despite being removed from the threatened species list, the whales still face threats as global warming warms our ocean waters, but this is a great example of how people can make changes that result in saving a species.

96. A retired forest engineer in Turkey turned a desert-like area of land into a lush forest after planting over 30 million trees in 25 years with the help of local villagers.

What was once a barren desert-like hill in a Turkish province along the Black Sea is now a lush forest of millions of trees. This was the result of work by a retired forest engineer named Hikmet Kaya and the local villagers who helped him. In a great story of determination, the people came together to transform the land by planting what is said to be over 30 million trees over the course of a 25-year period.

The villagers worked together to plant saplings that today continue to grow into a large forest. The creation of a forest has had an effect on the local climate and creates a habitat for new life to exist. Great work to all involved!

97. A sharp increase in the demand for renewable energy is causing Australia's largest coal-fired power plant to close seven years earlier than originally planned.

A nice surprise took place in Australia as consumer demand caused the closing of the country's largest coal-fired plant. The plant was expected to close in another seven years as a result of government action, but the plant owner moved to close it as there was not enough demand for its power given the availability and pricing of renewable energy alternatives.

The plant was recently responsible for 2% of all of Australia's greenhouse gas emissions, so its early closure is a big win for the environment. To top it all off, the operator is building a new battery in place of the coal plant, which will be capable of storing renewable energy as the country moves toward a brighter, renewable future. Great work, Australia.

98. Iceland has decided that whaling licenses will no longer be renewed once the last batch of them expire in 2023, finally ending the nation's commercial whaling industry.

In the past, whaling was a profitable industry as the world demanded whale products for cosmetics, meat, and oil. Iceland had a large commercial whaling industry as a result and issued licenses to companies to allow them to hunt whales for profit. Times have changed, however, as the global demand for whale products has declined dramatically as a result of education by conservationists. Now, Iceland's whaling industry has dramatically shrunk and will no longer be permitted once current licenses expire in 2023.

Activists have welcomed the news, and after nearly 30 years of campaigning for an end to Iceland's whaling industry, it appears that the job is complete!

99. Scotland announced that people under 22 years old can now travel on city buses for free.

In a move to tackle inequality, respond to climate change, and improve the lives of young people, Scotland announced that as of January 31, 2022, bus travel for people under age 22 will be free. Tens of thousands of young people have already applied for their free bus passes and many more are expected to apply over the coming months. The move adds to an already existing law that gives free bus travel to people over age 60 and disabled citizens. Altogether it means that over 2.3 million people in Scotland now have access to free bus transportation.

Increasing use of buses and other forms of public transit will help Scotland achieve its goal of reducing the number of miles traveled by car by 20% before the year 2030, as well as the goal of being a net-zero emissions country by the year 2045. Impressive!

100. Portugal is now a coal-free country after closing its last coal-fired power plant.

Portugal became the fourth country in Europe to be completely coal-free in terms of its power grid. The country reached this milestone nine years ahead of schedule!

    The movement away from burning coal to produce electricity is widespread, especially in Europe. Portugal joins Belgium, Austria, and Sweden as the four European countries to move completely away from this polluting form of energy.

101. After qualifying for the World Cup, the Serbian football (soccer) team donated its one million Euro ($1.13 million USD) prize to charities that help treat sick children in the country.

After beating Portugal 2-1 in a soccer match that earned them a bid to the 2022 World Cup, the Serbian soccer team celebrated by donating their $1.13 million prize to charities that help treat sick children in their country. The donation was received with great cheer from the local Serbian newspapers and media, with a headline that read, "Serbian football players pampered the nation again!"

102. A new law in Portugal aimed at improving the mental health of its people makes it so that your boss cannot call, email, or text you after work hours.

Work stress is one the most common sources of mental health issues among adults, and Portugal is trying to do something about it. The government passed a law that bans bosses from messaging staff after work hours. Under the new law, employers can face penalties if they contact staff outside of work hours and are not allowed to remotely monitor employees' work. Employers are also required to provide their employees with all the tools needed to do their work from home, including helping pay for their utility bills.

103. Over 100 countries have committed to stop and reverse deforestation by the end of the 2020s.

One hundred countries met at the COP26 summit in 2021 and agreed to end and reverse deforestation by the year 2030. The countries in the agreement represent over 85% of total forest coverage in the world, so it is seen as a big step toward helping reduce climate change.

The deforestation process contributes about 11% of the world's total CO2 emissions, so reversing the trend would have a massive impact in the fight against climate change. Some of the countries taking part include Canada, Russia, Brazil, Colombia, Indonesia, and Democratic Republic of the Congo, all of which have very large forests. Brazil is especially important since its forests include the incredibly important Amazon rainforest. The US and China will also be part of this agreement, showing that the world is together in the fight against climate change.

104. A massive new fishing-free area in the Pacific Ocean is being formed to create a "superhighway" for sea life.

Sharks, whales, turtles, and many other endangered species will soon have their own corridor where they can travel free from the threat of fishing. Four South and Central American countries agreed to combine their marine reserves to create the "Eastern Tropical Pacific Marine Corridor," an area in the ocean that covers more than 200,000 square miles. The area is one of the world's most important sea life migration routes and is part of an initiative to try to protect 30% of the planet's oceans from fishing by the year 2030.

While fishing is still an important part of the world's food supply, responsible fishing allows sea life to migrate along its usual routes, which can help increase reproduction and overall supplies of these fish for the planet. The "superhighway" is a great example of countries coming together to do responsible things for our environment.

105. Squirrels are a big help when it comes to the regeneration of oak forests, as they fail to recover 70% of the nuts they bury, which grow into trees.

Squirrels spend a large part of their days finding and burying nuts. While they do this for purposes of food storage, it has a positive unintended environmental effect as research suggests that they never recover a majority of the nuts they bury, which in turn can grow into trees and help with reforestation. Specifically, squirrels find acorns, which are the seeds of an oak trees, and bury them in the soil. The study, performed by the University of Richmond, found that up to 74% of these acorns are never unburied by the squirrels, which is likely responsible for the regeneration of oak forests.

Isn't nature amazing? What seems like a simple thing they do for food storage is in fact an important part of the ecosystem in which they live.

106. New York is testing a $1,000 per month income stipend for low-income first-time mothers to help them try to overcome poverty.

New York is one of the wealthiest cities in the world, yet nearly 25% of children under the age of three live in poverty there. A new program funded by the Monarch Foundation is attempting to fix that. The program is one of many recent trial programs that provides money to the needy on a consistent monthly basis as a form of income. Currently, they give first-time mothers who meet their low-income guidelines between $500 and $1,000 per month without any expectation that the money be repaid. Early reports on the status of the program show that it is helping mothers to establish childcare and buy their baby essential items that they would have otherwise gone without.

The concept of providing basic level income support to people in need is not new and has started to catch on in other places. The concept, often called Universal Basic Income, is that by providing a base level of money to people, we can help remove them from poverty and break the typical cycles that lead to generations of poverty that follow. In a world with as many resources as Earth, it is a realistic goal of humanity that no one live without basic needs like food, water, and housing.

107. A popular sandwich and burger condiment may also help us in the fight against climate change!

The airline industry is responsible for an estimated 2.5% of all carbon emissions in the United States. Globally, it is estimated that the airplane industry is responsible for 3.5% of all global warming. With airplanes being such a big cause of the climate problem, imagine if we could create a new kind of fuel that cut emissions from planes by 70%? Well, after four years of research that is exactly what researchers at the University of Georgia are trying to do.

The scientists say that a sustainable fuel made from the mustard plant has the potential to be created and would dramatically reduce the carbon footprint of flying. Even better news, a switch to mustard-based fuel would help grow an industry and lower the cost of fuel. With proper incentives, the researchers claim that this potential new mustard fuel could be produced at a price of less than a quarter of the cost of current petroleum-based fuels. A cheaper and cleaner fuel? Seems like a great idea!

108. Social media stars MrBeast and Mark Rober have launched an initiative aimed at removing 30 million pounds of trash from the oceans.

In 2021, two popular YouTube stars teamed up to raise $30 million in an effort to reduce trash from the world's oceans. The initiative, called #TeamSeas, pledged to remove one pound of trash for every $1 raised and has picked up significant traction online. It ended up picking up 62,738 lbs of plastic waste in four days. MrBeast raised $30 million USD in donations for the initiative.

109. Whales are a big help in reducing the amount of carbon in our atmosphere.

Scientists have discovered that whales store a huge amount of carbon dioxide, which, when it's their time to go, falls to the ocean floor with the whale, never to be seen again.

The impact of whales is actually thought to be quite large as one whale is estimated to store up to 33 tons of CO2 during their lifetime, which has the same effect that up to 1,000 trees can have in reducing carbon from the atmosphere. The effect is even larger when you take into account other sea life that rely on whales and contribute to our oxygen supply.

So, not only are whales majestic creatures to look at, but they are one of the Earth's great climate helpers.

110. The Gorilla Guardian Club is an organization that converts poachers into protectors by paying former hunters to monitor and protect the species they used to hunt.

Villagers in Cameroon have long earned a living by hunting gorillas (and other animals) and selling their catch to buyers. While it is hard to blame people for trying to make a living, the harm that poachers have to various animal life is large. Rather than using punishment to end their activities, a group in Cameroon has come up with an innovative way: pay the hunters to become protectors!

The club provides training and support to villagers who live near the rarest gorilla species, and then these villagers monitor the habitat and record signs of any threats that the species may be facing. The club also organizes various activities like storytelling, film showings, and events that involve children in the hopes of spreading the positive word of how magical these creatures are and why it is important to respect and protect wildlife.

111. Australia thinks that trees deserve an email address so that people can let them know how much they appreciate and love them!

The city of Melbourne gave email addresses to over 70,000 trees. The idea was meant to be so that people could send email reports about trees if there were any worrisome branches or other issues with the trees, but instead people are sending love letters and fan mail to the tree email addresses to let them know how much they appreciate them.

In an unintended but positive turn of events, the trees have received thousands of messages from all over the world as a sign of support for nature and the role that trees play in it. Letters often compliment the looks of the trees, their leaves and branches, as well as tell stories about how they have helped the trees in times of bad weather or fire. The organization responsible for the email address has even had some fun with it, writing back to some of the people that emailed the trees.

112. A half-mile-long barge and net system created by a nonprofit just took 20,000 pounds of plastic out of the ocean, proving that the garbage can be safely removed from our waterways.

A nonprofit called "The Ocean Cleanup" has invented a way to safely remove garbage from our oceans. The device, nicknamed "Jenny," is the latest invention by the organization after prior versions failed. Jenny was able to remove 20,000 pounds of garbage from the ocean and transport it back to landfills and recycling centers on land. Now, the organization believes that a fleet of 10 similar machines can clean up 50% of the trash in the Pacific garbage patch.

Years ago it was discovered that there is a garbage patch in the Pacific Ocean between California and Hawaii that is 1.6 million square kilometers (617,763 square miles), an area twice the size of Texas. Efforts like these are necessary to remove this tragic garbage patch and there is now renewed hope that it is indeed possible to do.

113. A major study finds that the ozone layer is healing and on pace for a full recovery by the year 2050.

In 1985, scientists noticed that the ozone layer, a layer of gas that deflects much of the sun's radiation from our environment, had a huge hole in it and was in danger of being completely eliminated within a few decades. If you have not heard much about it recently, that's because humanity has done a good job of saving ourselves from a disaster. Shortly after finding the hole in the ozone, scientists from all over the world banded together to identify the chemical that was causing the issue, and then countries worked together to ban it from use.

The efforts were a huge success as the existence of the harmful chemical went from 800,000 metric tons in the 1980s to 156 metric tons in 2014. The reduction in the use of this harmful chemical has resulted in not only stopping the decline of the ozone, but it has actually begun to regenerate and is on a path to recovery. Let this be a lesson that our collective action can change the course of climate history. As we battle the climate change emergency we are currently facing, the success we had in healing the ozone layer is a reminder that our efforts do matter and that we can win the fight.

114. In an effort to support the arts, Ireland announced a pilot program where they will pay over 2,000 artists a basic income to help support them.

Many of us appreciate the arts, and all of us have benefitted from them in some form or another, yet most artists struggle to make a living for themselves with their art. That is why the country of Ireland is establishing a pilot program to pay artists an income over a three-year period as a way to help support them and to show that their talent and work are appreciated.

The joy we often feel when experiencing culture and art goes a long way to helping us understand society and even ourselves. Supporting artists ensures that the arts are around for us and our children to enjoy.

115. Barn owls have replaced toxic pesticides in many California wineries as an alternative and natural way to protect grape vines and eliminate pests.

The farming industry has long used pesticides as a way to protect crops from insects that can harm them. Over the last decade, however, there has been a shift to try to eliminate many of these pesticides as many have been found to cause harm to humans when consumed and/or to the environment when used. The wine industry in California is one that has taken a leadership role as 80% of winemakers who used to rely on toxic pesticides are now using barn owls to do the job of protecting crops. Owls are a natural deterrent for rodents and keeping barn owls in the vineyard has become the primary choice of rodent control for winemakers.

Barn owls eat rodents during their four-month nesting season, when the owls spend roughly one-third of their time hunting in the vineyards. Nature solving nature!

Environment

116. The world's largest plastic recycling factory is opening in Sweden.

Plastic waste has long been a major problem for our environment. While limiting the use of plastic is the best solution to eliminate its pollution, recycling is another good way to ensure that we reduce the amount of plastic waste that reaches our oceans and landfills. Sweden is leading the world in this area as they are set to open the world's largest plastic recycling plant. The factory will be able to recycle all of the plastic used in Swedish households. The factory itself was designed to be a zero-emissions facility, meaning it will not pollute while performing the recycling.

The factory is being built by a group of Sweden-based trade groups and companies and will be the most modern facility of its kind. It will be capable of recycling up to 200,000 metric tons of plastic per year and will be operated by renewable energy from solar panels that cover the factory's roof. Great job, Sweden!

117. In 2021, a groundbreaking vaccine for malaria was approved and later rolled out to billions of people worldwide.

Malaria, a disease often transmitted by mosquito bites, is the biggest cause of childhood illness and death in sub-Saharan Africa. Numerous charitable organizations have been funding all sorts of solutions, from mosquito nets to education. While those have had a positive impact in reducing the amount of death and illness caused by malaria, no bigger solution is thought to exist than the potential for a malaria vaccine. After years of research, it appears that the world may have reached a positive turning point in the battle against malaria as a vaccine has been recommended by the World Health Organization after successful trials in Ghana, Kenya, and Malawi.

This marks a historic scientific breakthrough in the area of child health and malaria control as a malaria vaccine, in addition to existing prevention methods, has the potential to save tens of thousands of young lives each year. A great example of how wonderful science can be.

118. Australia's oldest surviving tropical rain forest has been given back to the Eastern Kuku Yalanji people, its Indigenous owners.

The Daintree is a tropical forest in Australia that is thought to be one of the oldest in the world. It borders the Great Barrier Reef and is part of the UNESCO World Heritage site. The Daintree and the Kuku Yalanji people have long had a history together and now more than 400,000 acres of land is being returned to the people to protect and share with visitors.

Australia has one of the oldest and largest indigenous populations in the world, and the return of the Daintree marks the first time that ownership of a national park has been returned to the natives. The return is a result of over four years of negotiations between the Kuku Yalanji people and the Australian government, but they have struck a deal!

119. Barcelona, Spain, is giving citizens who give up their gas-powered car three years of free public transportation.

While there are many methods to help fight climate change, reducing the number of gas-powered cars from the road is one of the most impactful methods of doing so. That is why a new program in Barcelona is being celebrated as it aims to incentivize citizens to use public transportation and eliminate gas-powered cars from the roads.

   The program provides a "T-Green" card to people who give up their car. The card can be used on all public transportation in the city and has already been claimed by over 12,000 people. The card is valid for three years and has already led to the removal of over 10,000 cars and almost 2,000 motorcycles from the streets. Not only is the program good for the environment, but it helps reduce noise and traffic pollution as it results in fewer cars being on the road than would otherwise be the case.

120. While there are thought to be only 73 southern resident wild orcas alive, in 2021 scientists discovered that three of them were pregnant!

Killer whales reproduce very slowly, so it is very difficult to save the species and have it grow back from near extinction. That is why the discovery that three of the wild orcas are pregnant is such a big deal to marine biologists (and the planet).

The pregnancies were discovered by two marine biologists who were on a trip in the waters of the Pacific Northwest. The news raises hopes of a potential turning point in the fight to keep these majestic creatures around for the future.

121. Spain announced that, beginning in 2023, it will ban single-use plastic wrap used to package fruits and vegetables.

In an effort to reduce waste and plastic pollution, Spain is banning the use of plastic wrap used by supermarkets to package fruits and vegetables. Starting in 2023, these single-use plastics will no longer be permitted, which is expected to help eliminate up to 1.6 million tons of plastic waste each year. This ban is even more significant since this type of plastic is recycled less than 50% of the time, so it is a true contributor to plastic pollution and waste.

Microplastic contamination along the entire Spanish coast has become a growing problem that affects sea life and humans. The move by the Spanish government follows a similar ban in France and the government is considering further action that will discourage the use of plastic water bottles by installing more public water fountains. Spain is aiming to reduce the number of plastic bottles by 50% within the next 10 years and hopes to ensure that 100% of plastics used are recyclable. Way to lead on this important environmental issue, Spain!

122. Over 50 million people in 180 countries came together on World Cleanup Day to help improve the planet!

World Cleanup Day is meant to have people from all over the world gather together to help improve our planet. In 2021, over 50 million people answered the call and removed up to 280,000 tons of trash from alongside rivers, on beaches, and in forests. This momentous occasion just goes to show the power of the masses and what humanity can accomplish when it joins together and puts its mind toward solving some of our planet's issues.

Of all the countries involved in this day, Germany topped the list, as they are said to have held more than 900 organized events on World Cleanup Day. France also did a great job with over 600 events and Italy came in at more than 500.

123. In a huge win for animals, the European Parliament passed a resolution in 2021 to phase out animal testing in scientific experiments.

There is a long-time practice of using animals to test products before they are green-lit for use by humans. In a win for animal rights activists, the European parliament voted on a measure that will phase out animal experiments.

The resolution calls for deep changes to the way products are tested and recognizes that "preferential funding of non-animal methods across all EU research and innovation initiatives" will be required in order to shift current practices to ones that do not rely on animal testing.

124. The Romanian football federation has teamed up with local dog shelters to promote pet adoption.

In a move to drive awareness of the need for more pet adoptions, the Romanian football federation has partnered with local dog shelters to promote pet adoption. Before each match, players hold a rescue dog in their arms to drive awareness and to promote more adoptions. Players walk onto the soccer field with one of the rescue dogs, who will have their name tag on a handkerchief so that any viewer who would like to adopt them can know which dog they're interested in and request more information.

The federation has decided to focus on this initiative and so every match in the main league in Romania will have the pet adoption ceremony before kick-off.

125. Since the Paris Climate Agreement, 76% of planned coal power plants have been scrapped in favor of other power generation options.

The age of coal is coming to an end, thanks in large part to the 2015 Paris Climate Agreement, which made the phasing out of coal power plants a primary objective. Countries have been moving toward alternative energy sources to fill their electricity needs, including renewables like solar and wind. That's great news!

In total, 76% of the world's plans for future coal power plants have been nixed since the agreement was signed. This is an amazing step toward removing the world's reliance on this polluting form of energy as we look to tackle the climate change challenge we are facing.

126. Vegan leather? That's right, a manufacturer in London is turning tons of pineapple waste from the Philippines into sustainable leather.

Zero-waste and cruelty-free fashion is possible! That is what a textile maker in London is trying to prove. A company called Pinatex is turning pineapple waste into sustainable leather material that can be used in purses, keychains, and other manufactured goods. This innovative process solves multiple problems as it not only creates cruelty-free leather but also helps to turn our food waste problem into products that can be used and enjoyed.

Historically, pineapple leaves that are not consumed are either burned or sent to landfills. This process is harmful to the environment as it produces CO_2, methane, and other emissions. By using these byproducts to produce vegan leather, we save the world from some harmful emissions and, at the same time, help local farmers generate new revenue from the sale of these byproducts.

127. The UK will soon become the first country to ban the import and export of all products containing shark fins.

Sharks are a key species in the ecosystem of our oceans and their existence is essential for the continued health of our marine environment. Sharks have also long been a highly sought-after form of food in certain cultures, and shark fins have also been historically sold for use in all sorts of products.

Banning the importation of all shark fin products is a big one, as it would reduce the demand for shark fin and thereby reduce the incentive for the practice of finning to take place around the world. The effort is said to boost shark population numbers.

128. A nightclub in Glasgow is testing a new method of creating energy needed to power the venue . . . heat from people dancing!

A Scottish nightclub is testing an innovative way to generate the electricity it needs to power the lights and sound system that many of its customers come to enjoy. That method is using the body heat of the people dancing in the club to generate energy, which is then used to power the building. The trial of this new innovation is part of an annual climate summit that brings together countries from around the world to discuss climate change and explore ways to prevent further climate damage.

This innovative "renewable heating and cooling system" works by transforming heat emitted from dancers into energy by using pumps and fluids to capture the heat before pushing the heat into holes drilled beneath the nightclub. The heat can then be stored for use to either heat or cool the venue when needed. The energy is also used to power electricity, gas, lighting, and the sound system. The nightclub estimates that it will save 70 tons of CO_2 by relying on this novel form of energy. So go ahead and dance the night away, folks!

129. In an unlikely partnership, each time a new child is born in Wales, two trees are planted, one at home and one in Uganda.

As of 2021, more than 15 million trees have been planted in Uganda as part of a program that aims to combat climate change. The project is being managed by "Size of Wales," a leading climate charity. The idea is meant to help restore Mbale, a hilly area in Uganda that used to be a rich forest but has been ravaged by deforestation.

Each time a baby is born in Wales, a tree is planted in Mbale as well as in Wales. The newborn baby receives a certificate made of recycled paper to celebrate their contribution to the environment. The project also provides other eco-friendly materials to the Mbale villagers in hopes of promoting sustainable and environmentally responsible living. The program expects to continue to plant trees at a rate of three million a year in order to help solve the area's environmental challenges.

130. Mexico has banned animal testing for purposes of creating cosmetics, the first country in North America to outlaw the practice.

In 2021, Mexico became the first country in North America to pass a ban on testing cosmetics on animals. The ban received overwhelming support from the voting members of government and will also serve to ban the manufacturing, importing, and marketing of cosmetics that involved testing on animals not just in Mexico but anywhere else in the world. With the ban, Mexico joins 40 other countries in passing a ban on animal testing for cosmetics and puts pressure on the rest of the world to join in eliminating this practice.

Kudos to Mexico for passing such important legislation.

131. Peecycling is a trend that may sound strange but can actually save one of our most precious natural resources . . . water!

A company in France called Toopi Organics is hoping that human urine can be the way forward when it comes to eco-friendly fertilizers for crops. It turns out that urine is made up of 95% water and includes other compounds like nitrogen and potassium, which help plants grow. Each day large amounts of urine are produced at no cost, yet we flush this potentially precious resource down the drain instead of using it for something useful. On the flip side, farmers worldwide use fossil fuel–based fertilizers to help their plants grow, which are not only costly but can be harmful to the environment to both produce and use.

Imagine a world where the things we need for our plants to grow is provided naturally through using recycled urine as a primary fertilizer. That may be close to reality as an innovative microbiological process developed by Toopi Organics can transform human urine into fertilizers. The process has been tested in dozens of studies and the urine-based fertilizer has shown similar efficiency to synthetic fertilizers, and at a lower cost to the farmer.

The challenge is how to collect large quantities of urine in a clean and safe way, but the company is working on a number of products that can help do so and hopefully bring this strange but innovative solution to market.

FUREVER LOVE

132. A German animal shelter is using a dating app to create profiles of cats and dogs to match with their new home.

With so many abandoned pets in existence, an animal shelter in Germany has come up with a fun way to try to find new homes for their animals: by putting them on a dating service. That's right, the animal shelter found a marketing agency willing to do photo shoots of some of their animals. They then loaded the images onto a dating app so that humans who are looking for a furry companion could scroll through the pets, read their bios, and potentially adopt one.

The service allows humans to browse images of potential pet companions, and if they "swipe right" on a particular image it helps set up a "date" with the animal shelter for the person to meet their potential forever friend. "There aren't only lonely souls among humans, but there are also a lot of lonely souls among animals," said one of the organizers. Here's hoping this helps many cute animals find a new home!

133. In 1979, a 16-year-old boy began to plant one tree sapling per day in India. Forty years later, this boy has created a forest that is larger than New York's Central Park.

In an amazing story about how one person can change the world, and how a number of small tasks can add up to something huge, a new forest exists because of 40 years of work by a local boy in India.

At age 16, Jadav Payeng noticed that there were hundreds of dead animals as a result of extreme heat in a drought-stricken part of his country. He knew that without shade, many more animals would die in the heat. So he decided to try to do something about it and began to plant trees. Now, over 40 years later, a forest that covers 1,390 acres exists.

At first, planting trees was time-consuming with little to show for it, until the trees started to grow and then generated their own seeds. As the forest grew, it started to fill with birds, deer, rhinos, tigers, and many more animals seeking to enjoy its shade.

134. In an effort to stop illegal net fishing, an Italian activist has dropped marble statues into the sea, creating an artistic and effective way to halt the illegal practice of net fishing in the area.

In the Tuscan village of Talamone lived a boy who began fishing at age 13 and has continued to do so into his 60s. In recent years, however, his job became harder as illegal net fishing in the region destroyed the marine ecosystem. While local laws banned net fishing within three miles of the coast, it was such a profitable practice that many boats ignored the laws. To try to stop the practice, this fisherman asked a local quarry if they would donate marble in order for him to work with artists in sculpting statues. His idea was that he could then drop the statues into the sea, which would not only create an underground museum of statues but would also make it harder for net fisherman to use their nets near the coast. The marble statues break up the nets when they are used, which no longer makes net fishing practical.

What a creative way to use art to protect the marine ecosystem and help end a harmful fishing practice. Great work!

135. The Welsh government has suspended all future road-building plans in favor of promoting more sustainable transportation.

Buses, trains, and even bicycles are alternative transportation methods to gas-guzzling cars. The government of Wales has a plan to try to promote the uses of these methods. In 2021, the Welsh government announced that it is freezing new road building projects as part of its plan to tackle the climate emergency.

Shifting away from spending money on projects that encourage more people to drive is a great start and one we hope many countries follow.

136. Indigenous communities in the United States have rebounded over the last 100 years from a low population of 250,000 to the largest population in modern US history (almost 10 million).

In the late 1800s, as a result of wars and western expansion into the United States, Indigenous population numbers in the United States declined dramatically. Western expansion often included extermination, forced boarding schools, and land theft, and the numbers fell to only 250,000 officially counted Indigenous peoples in 1890. Since then, however, as a result of their resistance and legal battles over tribal sovereignty and civil rights, populations have rebounded to the largest size in modern US history. While the wrongs that were done to the Indigenous community can't be forgotten, it is good to see progress in trying to recover from those wrongs.

137. Amazing news from Kenya! After decades of declining rhino populations, no rhinos were poached in 2020.

Kenya saw an 11% increase in their rhino population since 2019, with over 1,600 rhinos tracked by conservationist groups. In 2015, the Kenya Wildlife Service put in place a monitoring system to track the rhino and elephant populations. The service helps scientists track endangered species, which they can also use to link the animals to suspected poachers. Historically, rhinos were a heavily poached animal. In recent years, however, efforts by conservationist groups including the Kenya Wildlife Service and the International Fund for Animal Welfare have helped keep the animals safe and free from poaching.

Hunting animals has caused many species to become extinct or close to extinct, but as we evolve as a species and realize the value of diverse creatures on our planet, we continue to make great strides in protecting species from the risk of extinction. And that is great news!

138. The secret to a long life? One town in Italy credits fresh air, good food, books, and no arguing.

As of 2021, a small village on the island of Sardinia is home to 13 times more people who are 100 years old or older—much higher than Italy's national average. In total, there are 534 people who are 100 or older in Sardinia, which represents 33.6 people for every 100,000. What is the secret to a long life? A local professor believes that fresh air, good food, and the locals' approach to stress are the main factors. These centenarians went through wars, hunger, and other difficulties, but they managed to adapt. If there was a problem, they found ways to solve it.

Some of the locals believe that reading, walking, playing cards, and a proper diet are the key factors.

No matter the reason, it is surely an interesting thing for researchers to study as Sardinia appears to have found the fountain of youth.

139. Need a mood boost? Nibbling on dark chocolate can improve your mood thanks to its high amount of antioxidant flavonoids.

The mood-boosting effects of chocolate have been known for a long time, but recent research also shows a link between dark chocolate and managing anxiety. Cocoa has the highest concentration of flavonoids among commonly consumed foods and scientists have found that certain flavonoids have antihistamine, antimicrobial, and even memory- and mood-enhancing properties.

Low serotonin is one of the leading causes of anxiety and dark chocolate provides large amounts of tryptophan, an amino acid that also works as a precursor to serotonin. So, the thinking is that by ingesting more dark chocolate, a person can improve their serotonin levels, which helps with anxiety. Another ingredient in chocolate is theobromine, which studies have shown can have a positive, mood-elevating effect.

Not only is dark chocolate delicious, but it can have a positive effect on your mental health!

Environment

140. Madrid is planting Europe's largest metropolitan forest to help combat climate change.

In 2021, a 47-mile-long green wall that will cut CO2 emissions by 175,000 tons per year was announced to be planted and built in Madrid, Spain. The effort is one that authorities in the country are undertaking to help combat climate change and city pollution and, when complete, will become Europe's largest metropolitan forest. Called "El Bosque Metropolitano" (the Metropolitan Forest), the project will include over 450,000 trees and related vegetation, which will include new parks, dog trails, hiking and biking routes, and other outdoor areas to service local residents and tourists alike. The trees and vegetation being planted will include native species such as olive trees, ash, rosemary, and many more bushes and shrubs.

Not only is tree planting a good way to help remove CO2 from the environment, but it beautifies the city and gives people a place to enjoy our great planet.

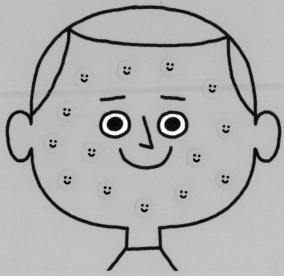

141. Kindness is contagious! Start a chain of kindness with a kind act that will encourage others to do the same.

When you either see or do an act of kindness, you (or the people that see you) are likely to follow suit. This has been studied by researchers at Stanford University. Kindness creates a self-perpetuating cycle that can make other people happier, healthier, and more connected to their environment and the people inside it. The domino effect of acts of kindness can go a long way toward promoting empathy and improving society as a whole.

    We all need a little more kindness right now, but we can't just want it to happen, we need to make it happen. More kindness in our families, our communities, and our world. It's time to plant that seed.

142. More than 180 publicly out LGBTQ+ athletes competed in the Tokyo Olympics in 2021, smashing a global record.

Representation matters! That is why it was such a significant event when over 180 publicly out LGBTQ+ athletes competed in the Olympic Games held in Tokyo in late summer 2021. Delayed by a year because of the COVID-19 pandemic, the Tokyo Olympics served as a little bit of healing for a society that had been locked down, and also served as a monumental milestone for human rights and the right to be represented. A record-setting 186 members of the LGBTQ+ community participated in the Tokyo Olympics, which was more than twice the count at the 2016 Olympics and represented more openly LGBTQ+ athletes than all other Summer Olympics combined. Twenty-seven countries in 26 sports had representation, with the United States leading the way with 30 athletes, followed by Canada and Britain.

Representation of all communities is key to fostering understanding and reducing hate driven by the fear of the unknown or unrelatable. Kudos to the athletes for all their hard work at the Games.

143. Basel, Switzerland, has become the first city in the world to make green roofs mandatory on new buildings.

Inner-city green spaces have tremendous benefits to the environment and the society that lives within it. Green spaces help with climate change but also improve both the mental and physical health of those around them. To help drive more green spaces in their country, Switzerland came up with a plan that has resulted in almost 11 million square feet of green spaces being planted in the unlikeliest of places—building rooftops. That's right, an initiative driven by the local government has mandated that all new buildings must include patches of green space on the rooftops to help cool buildings off quicker during the summer months.

The new law is part of Basel's biodiversity strategy, and while rooftop green spaces have been required for all retrofitted buildings for 15 years already, the new laws require even more and is helping to make Basel the leading city in "greening" its urban spaces.

144. In 2021, Greenland announced that it will halt all new oil and gas endeavors.

After years of protest and lobbying by dedicated climate activists and government officials, Greenland has moved to ban all new oil and gas exploration efforts. Citing the escalating climate emergency and concerns for the arctic environment on which Greenland relies, the government made the announcement and called it necessary to expedite the transition away from fossil fuels. Way to go, Greenland!

145. Chile is creating the world's first constitution to be drafted by an equal number of men and women.

Setting a new global standard for gender equality, Chile has decided to have its new constitution drafted by an equal number of men and women. Women's rights activists in the country are proud to contribute to the new document, which will catalyze progress for women in the country and could set a new global standard for gender equity in politics.

Despite being a democratic country since 1990, Chile has been driven by a largely male political class and, with the Catholic church still wielding a lot of local influence in policy-making, the country has been slow to improve the representation of women in government. That is set to change as Chileans will elect a 150-person assembly to write a new constitution that is sure to be one of the most representative documents in the world. You go, girls!

146. The city of Leicester in the United Kingdom is installing a new network of "bee bus stops" that will be topped with a mix of flowers to encourage pollination.

The city of Leicester in the United Kingdom has come up with a clever plan to help revive the local bee population, using wasted space at bus stops to plant bee gardens!

Working with advertising firm Clear Channel to fund the development of these bee bus stops, the roofs will be planted with a mix of wildflowers that can attract pollinating insects while at the same time helping to beautify the city. The local government says that these bee bus stops will also help absorb rainwater falling on the roof among other positive environmental impacts. Isn't this idea the bee's knees?

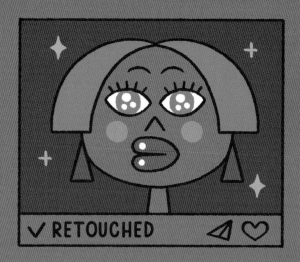

147. To combat beauty and appearance pressures, Norway has passed a law that requires social media influencers to disclose when they've retouched or added a filter to a photo.

Social media has long been blamed for an increase in pressures relating to body image and perceived beauty among teens. Some studies suggest that social media usage increases the likelihood of depression, eating disorders, and other mental health problems. Celebrities, brands, and even regular users with access to filters often touch up their photos, which causes an unedited person to think that they do not look as good as these touched-up images do. To combat the problem, Norway is now requiring celebrities, social media influencers, and brands to mark any image that is altered with an "edited" tag so that the casual observer knows that the image has been doctored. Transparency is key!

148. Plant-based food sales are growing at a faster rate than the animal products they aim to replace.

The Good Food Institute reported that plant-based food sales are up 54% since 2018, and in 2021 their growth rate was higher than their animal-based counterparts. The report stated that the plant-based food industry hit $7.4 billion in sales in the United States, a 54% growth rate, which is especially impressive when the growth rate of food sales in general was only 2%. Impressive!

The report found that plant-based eggs are the fastest-growing vegan food category, and plant-based creamers and ready-to-drink beverages are also growing at over 20% per year. A move to plant-based products is a win for animal rights activists and the environment, as the negative impact on the environment from plant-based products is far less than that of animal products. The continued growth of this category of food has eliminated concerns that there was no market for plant-based products, and it is now realistic to think that they will someday be a larger market category than animal products.

149. Worm delivery? A company in the UK delivers worms to your mailbox for use in your home composting bin to help eliminate food waste.

You've heard of home-delivered food, clothes, and toys, but have you ever had home-delivered worms? That is what a UK company has started to do and there is a good reason for it: to encourage home composting. At-home composting is great for the environment as it helps eliminate rotting food waste, which releases greenhouse gases such as methane and nitrous oxide. By feeding food waste to worms, the food is broken down naturally before any of the harmful gases are released into the environment. Worms also use that food to consume nutrients that are later good for the soil in which they live.

The company has 1,000 packs of tiger worms ready to be delivered to schools, community groups, and households who want to help the environment by composting at home. The delivery even comes with instructions on how to create your own worm farm.

150. "Koe Knuffelen," or cow hugging, is a fun trend noted in the Netherlands to reduce stress.

Cow hugging is a unique self-care practice in the Netherlands that is based on the old-fashioned promise of a good human-to-animal snuggle. Patrons wishing to practice this technique typically take a tour of the cow farm and finish the tour by resting against one of the cows. Practitioners say that the cow's warmer body temperature, slower heartbeat, and large size make hugging them a soothing experience. Cow cuddling is also believed to boost oxytocin in humans, the hormone released in social bonding, and the commonly known calming effects of a support animal are said to be enhanced when involving larger mammals. Who doesn't want to try this?

 the_happy_broadcast

 happybcast

 @thehappybroadcast

About Mauro & Keith

Mauro Gatti is originally from Italy and currently lives in Los Angeles, California. Mauro is an illustrator, designer, and award-winning creative director who loves food (pizza is his top choice), animals, and all things creative. Mauro uses his artistic talents to try to bring a little bit of happiness to those around him. He believes that kindness and smiles can go a long way to helping improve society as a whole, as small actions by many can add up to make a big impact.

Keith Bonnici is originally from Malta and now lives in Los Angeles with his wife, Monique, and their three young boys, Luca, Dominic, and Lorenzo. Keith used to be a lawyer before becoming an entrepreneur and, a few years ago, sold his company so that he can now focus on passion projects that he hopes can help make the world a better place for his children. Keith has lived in Europe, Asia, and the United States, and enjoys traveling, socializing with friends, and anything sports related. He also has a passion for new technologies that can have a positive impact on society.

Acknowledgments

Plenty of people were involved in the creation of this book, namely, the amazing people who are doing all the wonderful things for our world that we write and draw about. There were plenty of talented helpers that lent a hand in writing and editing this book, including Jaidon Gupta and Dhilon Gupta, brothers and sophomore students at La Cañada High School, and Luca Bonnici, an eighth grader at St. Bedes Elementary School and incoming freshman at St. Francis High School.

We also want to thank the many people who have helped build The Happy Broadcast and WHOLE into what it is today, including our talented TikTok leader Elisheva Glaser, design star and good friend Daniele Codega, our amazing app developer Nico Cavallin, the artist behind our Solmate project Davide Saraceno, talented animator Stefano Meazza, longtime supporter Francio Ferrari, all our investors and advisors, and Mauro's best four-legged friend Cyrus (RIP).